ABOUT THE BOOK

The author skillfully brings to light little-known facts that will increase your understanding and appreciation of God's written Word. You'll find a discussion of how the Bible has been preserved through countless generations; you'll be amazed by the efforts throughout history to silence the voice of today's best seller — the Bible. If it were "just another book," would the Bible maintain its universal influence or transform the lives of people who study it? You'll find the material in this book is some of the most interesting reading about the Bible that you've enjoyed in a long time.

ABOUT THE AUTHOR

The author, James C. Hefley, is a full-time, free-lance writer in the religious field. This is his thirteenth book to be published. Some of his other books are: *Scientists Who Believe* and *Businessmen Who Believe* (David C. Cook Publishing Co.); *Living Miracles* (selected for the White House Library), *Play Ball, Sports Alive, Illustrated,* and *Adventurers with God* (Zondervan Publishing House).

In preparing *What's So Great About the Bible,* Mr. Hefley utilized his special studies in Greek, Hebrew, Biblical archaeology, and Biblical textual criticism; and his travels to primitive tribes where the Wycliffe Bible Translators are at work.

WHAT'S SO GREAT

ABOUT THE BIBLE

JAMES C. HEFLEY

DAVID C. COOK PUBLISHING CO.
Elgin, Illinois

WHAT'S SO GREAT ABOUT THE BIBLE

© 1969 David C. Cook Publishing Co., Elgin, Illinois 60120

Printed by PYRAMID PUBLICATIONS,
    for David C. Cook Publishing Co.

Printed in the United States of America.

Library of Congress Catalog Card Number: 77-87317

Dedicated to the myriad Bible translators, publishers, and distributors who have made it possible for the Bible to be read in almost 1300 languages.

WHAT'S SO GREAT
ABOUT THE BIBLE

PREFACE

The Bible contains a blueprint for the Church and for democratic constitutions. The Bible provides the key to unlock life's most puzzling questions and reveals the road to Heaven. The Bible is the Book of the small and great, rich and poor, president and peasant, scholar and student. It is read in Borneo and Baghdad, in Djakarta and Detroit, in El Salvador and Ethiopia. Sophisticated suburbanites and tattooed tribesmen study it with equal interest.

Abraham Lincoln read the Bible in the early morning hours and said a year before his death, "Take all this Book you can upon reason and the balance upon faith, and you will live and die a better man."

Today 800,000,000 people profess to follow the teachings of the Bible; 115,000,000 in the United States alone. Almost 400,000 United States clergymen will preach two to three billion sermons this year, using the Bible as their major source and authority. Over 3,000,000 Sunday school teachers in America will give one and one-half billion lessons from the Bible to more than 40,000,000 students. Billions of written materials — books, religious magazines, church newspapers, and tracts — will be published about the Bible.

The Bible is the most widely read and circulated book there is, yet few people know the amazing facts behind the writing, translation, preservation, influence, and power of the Bible. The purpose of *What's So Great About the Bible* is to present the Bible as the Book above all books.

Appreciation is expressed to the AMERICAN BIBLE SOCIETY and THE WYCLIFFE BIBLE TRANSLATORS for providing photographs and factual information from their libraries.

—JAMES C. HEFLEY

CONTENTS

List of Illustrations

CHAPTER 1

IT'S A LITERARY MIRACLE

As a "literary miracle" the Bible holds no peer. That it ever was a book — and is today The Book — for every man, is truly a miracle. Compare the writing of the Bible to the writing of any ordinary book. In the preparation of most books, the author has an idea or is assigned a topic. He thinks the idea through, makes an outline, confers with editors, and collects research material. Then he writes or dictates the book and sends it to a publisher. In this process as much as two years may have elapsed. There are exceptions, of course. Some books have been assigned, written, and published in a matter of months. Some books have been written in prisons and smuggled out to a publisher in another country. Some have been written after a lifetime of thinking and planning. But no book has ever duplicated the production schedule of the Bible.

Except in the mind of God, there never really was a production schedule. A group of writers and editors did not sit down in the beginning and plan the 66 books of the Bible. More than 40 different writers and editors (many of them non-scholars) worked on the Bible, but their work spanned 60 generations. Think of it — a book with its beginning and end written 1,500 years apart!

Without committee planning, the Bible grew part by part, book by book, century by century, in an orderly, progressive manner.

First there was only The Law, commonly called the "Pentateuch," or the "First Five Books of Moses." When David took the throne in Israel, there were few additional records of sacred history available. During David's and Solomon's time, the Bible grew more rapidly, and finally — one by one — the prophecies were recorded to complete the Jewish Old Testament.

The New Testament was written in a much shorter time — about half a century. But here also there was no prearranged plan made in a conference of writers. Matthew, Mark, Luke, and John did not form a committee and agree that Matthew emphasize Christ as King, Mark show Him as the Worker, Luke present Him as the Man, and John proclaim Him as the Son of God.

Paul and James did not meet on the road to Jerusalem and decide that Paul should dwell on doctrine and James write on practical morals. John and Peter did not hold an island retreat and plan for John to write about the future in symbolic language, while Peter addressed encouragement to persecuted Christians.

No Editorial Plan

There was no human editorial plan in writing the Bible. The Biblical writers and editors prepared their manuscripts as moved by the Holy Spirit (II Peter 1:20, 21). The authors wrote to reflect on lessons they had learned (Solomon in Proverbs), to express deep spiritual feelings (David in the Psalms), to record the expansion of the early church (Luke in Acts), to advise the church on serious problems (Paul in I Corinthians), to give practical instruction in Christian living (James in his epistle), and so on.

They wrote in three different languages (Hebrew, Aramaic, and Greek), in many countries, and under varying circumstances. Parts of the Bible were written in palaces, other parts in prisons. Most of the Bible was produced in Palestine, but much was written in Babylon, Rome, Asia Minor, Greece, and perhaps even Arabia. The Old Testament manuscripts were probably written on dried animal skins; the New Testament on papyrus.

The Biblical journalists used different styles to produce various types of literature. Biography, theology, philosophy, poetry, prophecy, genealogy, ethnology, romance, adventure, and travel are all found in the Bible.

And yet — though the Bible is a literary garden in style, authorship, topics, and languages — its 66 books are a marvelous unit. The 66 books are a perfect whole, a purposeful revelation, a progressive proof that the Bible is more than the work of fallible men.

God's Message to Man

The Bible begins with God (Genesis 1:1) and ends with man, the climax and crown of all God's work (Revelation 22:21). In between, the Bible is God's inspired message to man, having as its purpose to bring man to God.

God's message is presented progressively on the tablets of history. From the first couple is descended a people that grew into a chosen nation, intended to be God's instrument of blessing to all mankind. From the nation of Israel came the Messiah, God Incarnate, the Savior of all mankind. From the Savior's redemptive work comes the Church, God's spiritual body in which He dwells and will carry out His purposes to the end of time.

The parts of the Bible are connected by the message of the whole. The separate books are related by the revelation of one God. The Old Testament and the New Testament are hinges on the one door that opens into the presence of God.

18

The Testaments complement rather than contradict each other. The Old Testament predicts Christ; the New Testament proclaims the Savior.

The Old Testament is a highway of Messianic prophecy running often through dark valleys, but flowing into the New Testament which reveals Jesus as the Light of the World.

As an unknown poet wrote:

> The New is in the Old concealed;
> The Old is in the New revealed;
> The New is in the Old contained;
> The Old is in the New explained.

Ouvier, a famous French anatomist, said that a complete organism can be determined by three laws: (1) each part must be essential to the whole; (2) each part must be related or correspond to the other parts as in the human body; and (3) all parts must be pervaded by the spirit of life.

The Bible meets all these requirements. Each part of the Bible is essential to the whole; the parts of the Bible are related to each other; and the spirit of life is present because the Bible bears the message of the living God.

Bible Claims to Be Inspired

Volumes have been written to explain how the Bible was inspired of God. Perhaps we should first consider what the Bible says about itself.

There are only three examples in the Bible of

Deity writing: (1) the Ten Commandments were written on tablets of stone "with the finger of God" (Exodus 31:18; 32:16); (2) the writing on Belshazzar's wall (Daniel 5:5); (3) the writing of Jesus on the ground when the sinful woman was brought before Him (John 8:6, 8).

The actual word "inspiration" occurs only twice in the whole Bible. The first time is in Job 32:8 and may not refer to the Scriptures. The second instance is in II Timothy 3:16 and definitely does refer to Scripture. "All Scripture is given by inspiration of God and is profitable for doctrine, for reproof, for correction, for instruction in righteousness." The word "inspiration," which means literally in Greek "breathed by God," is translated from the compound Greek word, *theopneustos* — *theo* ("God") and *pneustos,* from the verb *pneo* ("to breathe"). *Pneustos* includes more than just wind or physical breath in its meaning. It incorporates the vital principle and the spirit by which one feels, thinks, wills, and decides.

It is generally held that God in inspiring His Word, guided the spirits by which His spokesmen felt, thought, and decided what to write. God did not rob His writers of their styles or personalities, but He did guide their thought processes as they wrote. John, for example, wrote very simple Greek, whereas Dr. Luke used many medical and classical words in his writings.

20

Many theories of inspiration have been proposed. (See the Bibliography on page 91 for a list of books to aid in further study of these.) More than insight and illumination were involved in Biblical inspiration, although the Biblical writers did write from deep experiences with God.

Testimony of Scholars

What are some of the things Christian students and scholars through the ages have said about God's Book?

Clement of Rome (about A.D. 90): "The Scriptures are the true words of the Holy Spirit."

Tertullian (155-225): "The Scriptures are the writings of God."

Origen (185-254): "There is not one jot or one tittle written in Scripture which, for those who know how to use the power of the Scriptures, does not affect its proper work."

Augustine (354-430): "I have learned to pay them (the books of Scripture) such honor and respect as to believe most firmly that not one of their authors has erred in writing anything at all."

Martin Luther (1483-1546): "No other doctrine should be proclaimed in the church than the pure word of God, that is, the Holy Scriptures."

Louis Gaussen (1790-1863): "Inspiration is that inexplicable power which the Divine Spirit put forth of old on the authors of Holy Scripture."

Benjamin B. Warfield (1851-1921): "Inspiration is that extraordinary, supernatural influence exerted by the Holy Ghost on the writers of our Sacred Books, by which their words were rendered also the words of God, and, therefore, perfectly infallible."

Edward J. Young (contemporary): "Inspiration is a superintendence of God the Holy Spirit over the writers of the Scriptures, as a result of which these Scriptures possess Divine authority and trustworthiness and . . . are free from error."

Billy Graham (contemporary): "Either God did speak to these men as they wrote by inspiration, or they were the most consistent liars the earth ever saw. To tell more than 2,000 lies on one subject seems incredible, and more than 2,000 times the writers of the Bible said that God spoke these words!"

Testimony of Scripture

Scripture testifies for itself in hundreds of places. There are more than 2,600 instances in the Old Testament where the Scriptures claim to be "God's words." "The Lord said," "God spake," "These are the words of the Lord," "The Lord commanded," and like expressions occur again and again in Scripture.

Jesus upheld the claims of the Old Testament writers. Referring to the Jewish Scriptures, He asked, "Have ye not read that which was spoken unto you by God?" (Matthew 22:31). Jesus also declared, "Verily I say unto you, Till heaven and earth pass, one jot or one tittle shall in no wise pass from the law, till all be fulfilled" (Matthew 5:18).

Peter said, "For the prophecy came not in old time by the will of man: but holy men of God spake as they were moved by the Holy Ghost" (II Peter 1:21).

In addition to these testimonies there are other important witnesses to the inspiration of the Bible. One is fulfilled prophecy. The Old Testament prophets predicted, anticipated, and expected. They proclaimed prophecies about Israel, Egypt, Assyria, Babylon, and other foreign countries, prophecies that were fulfilled many years later.

Testimony of Fulfilled Prophecy

Centuries before Christ was born, His ancestry (Isaiah 9:7), birthplace (Micah 5:2), manner of birth (Isaiah 7:14), infancy (Hosea 11:1), manhood (Isaiah 40:11), character (Isaiah 9:6), career (Isaiah 35:5,6), reception (Zechariah 9:9), rejection (Micah 5:1), death (Psalm 22:16), burial (Isaiah 53:9), resurrection (Psalm 16:10), and ascension (Psalm 68:18) were all prophesied and written down. By inspiration, the Old Testament writers drew a picture of a man not yet born, a feat that has no equal.

Dr. A. Kurt Weiss, a Jewish professor at the University of Oklahoma Medical School, says regarding his conversion, "I came to believe that Christ was the One predicted by the prophets of my people."

A college class in the Pasadena (California) City College applied the laws of probability to the fulfillment of eight Old Testament prophecies concerning the coming of Christ. They concluded:

(1) birth in Bethlehem (Micah 5:2) — one chance in 280,000; (2) a forerunner or messenger would announce His coming (Malachi 3:1) — one chance in 1,000; (3) the Messiah would make a triumphant entry into Jerusalem upon a colt (Zechariah 9:9) — one chance in 10,000; (4) He would be betrayed by a friend and suffer wounds (Zechariah 13:6) — one chance in 1,000; (5) the betrayer would receive 30 pieces of silver (Zechariah 11:12) — one chance in 10,000; (6) the silver would be thrown to a potter (Zechariah 11:13) — one chance in 100,000; (7) the Savior, though innocent, would be oppressed and afflicted; He would make no defense (Isaiah 53:7) — one chance in 10,000; and (8) He would die by crucifixion (Psalm 22:16) — one chance in 10,000.

Based on these estimates, the class figured that the chance of all eight of these prophecies being fulfilled by one person would be the equivalent of 280,000 $\times$ 1,000 $\times$ 10,000 $\times$ 1,000 $\times$ 10,000 $\times$ 100,000 $\times$ 10,000 $\times$ 10,000.

Testimony of Archaeology

The testimony of the archaeologists' spade also attests to the inspiration of the Bible. Excavators have taken us back into the ages, countries, and living situations of the Biblical writers. The Old Testament record does not stand alone; other ancient records now offer additional support to Old Testament claims. We now have, for example, Indian, Persian, Greek, and Chaldean stories of a great Flood. Diggings at Ur of the Chaldees prove that the Biblical story of Abraham was written in keeping with the character and culture of that time.

Many criticisms that the Old Testament is historically inaccurate have been refuted by the spade. One example is the Hittites, mentioned over 40 times in the Old Testament.* Critics claimed that the Hittites never existed — until Hittite monuments were uncovered in the Middle East. Today, the existence of the Hittites is acclaimed as historical fact.

There are thousands of names, dates, places, and events mentioned in the Bible. Not all have been confirmed. But through archaeology many problems

* Genesis 15:20; 23:10; 26:34; 36:2 and others.

have been solved, many obscure texts have been clarified, and some so-called contradictions have been cleared up. The case for Biblical accuracy has been strengthened from the viewpoint of human reason.

Testimony of Scientific Accuracy

There is also the witness of scientific facts stated in the Bible, unknown and unaccepted when they were written, but known today to be accurate.

Centuries before Harvey proclaimed his theory of the circulation of the blood, the Bible declared, "The life of the flesh is in the blood" (Genesis 9:4; Leviticus 17:11; and others).

As late as the time of George Washington, people believed in bloodletting — taking blood from the bodies of the seriously ill — as a curative for every disease. While phlebotomy (bloodletting) is still used effectively in the treatment of some diseases, physicians today realize that excessive loss of blood weakens the body. Actually, in most instances, effort is expended to control excessive bleeding as a means of saving life.

Ancient peoples commonly believed the earth was flat. Copernicus and Columbus were mocked. But Isaiah 40:22 speaks of the Lord sitting on the circle of the earth.

The ancients also thought the earth was held in place by some under-support. But Job 26:7

declares, "He stretcheth out the north over the empty place, and hangeth the earth upon nothing." Some scholars debate whether or not this verse anticipates modern astronomy; some conservative scholars strongly suggest that it does.

The apostle John saw a vision of "four angels standing on the four corners of the earth" (Revelation 7:1). For centuries the idea of a four-cornered earth was ridiculed. But no more! Measurements by space-age satellites have demonstrated John's statement to be accurate. The satellites were pulled downward at the center of four high points or "corners" by unexpectedly high gravity.

Job, probably the oldest of all Biblical books, speaks of how "the morning stars sang together" (Job 38:7). Thinkers once said this was impossible. Now we know there is a unity in the natures of light and sound. Many light properties are wave motions. Could our ears operate at the right frequency, we might hear the melody in the color coming from the stars of different temperatures and therefore, different colors.

Jeremiah declared, "the host (stars) of heaven cannot be numbered" (Jeremiah 33:22). The scientist Hipparchus, a Greek astronomer who lived a few hundred years after Jeremiah, said, "There are only 1,056 stars in the heavens. I have counted them." A few hundred years after Hipparchus, another scientist, Ptolemy, counted 1,056 stars and agreed that was all. Not until A.D. 1610 did Galileo look through a telescope and proclaim, "There are many more stars." Modern astronomers estimate 100 billion stars hang in our galaxy alone.

Paul wrote in I Corinthians 15:41, "One star differeth from another star in glory." Many may look alike to the naked eye, but modern astronomers have photographed millions of stars and found no two alike.

Man Yearns for God

Perhaps the best witness of all is the testimony within man that tells him the Bible is the Book of God. No one needs proof that the sun shines, or that roses give off fragrance. No one doubts the power of love, and the beauty of good music. As Pascal, a great scientist and devout Christian, has said, "There are truths that are felt and there are truths which are proved. Principles are felt; propositions are proved. The heart has reasons, which the reason does not know."

To which Henry Van Dyke added, "After all, the Bible must be its own argument and defense. The power of it can never be proved unless felt. The authority of it can never be supported unless it is manifest. The light of it can never be demonstrated unless it shines."

In the same vein, the noted counselor, Dr. Frank Crane, wrote, "In that final hour that comes to all men . . . this Book alone brings the word, like a bell in the fog, of Him who says, 'I am the resurrection and the Life' " (John 11:25).

When Sir Walter Scott was dying, he asked his son-in-law to read to him out of the Book. "What book?" the younger man asked. Scott replied weakly but confidently, "There is only *one* Book, the Bible."

After his death, these verses were found written in Scott's Bible:

> *Within that awful volume lies*
> *The mystery of mysteries!*
> *Happiest they of human race,*
> *To whom God has granted grace.*
>
> *To read, to fear, to hope, to pray,*
> *To lift the latch, and force the way,*
> *And better had they ne'er been born,*
> *Who read to doubt, or read to scorn.*

CHAPTER 2

IT REMAINS UNCHANGED

Voltaire, the noted French infidel, boasted, "One hundred years from my day there will not be a Bible in the earth except one that is looked upon by an antiquarian curiosity-seeker." Two hundred years later a first edition of Voltaire's work sold in Paris for eleven cents. That same day—Christmas Eve, 1933—the British Government paid the Soviet government $500,000 for an ancient Biblical manuscript. This manuscript, *Codex Sinaiticus*, dating to about A. D. 350, was found in 1844 and is now in the British Museum. It is referred to by modern scholars in translating the Bible into modern languages.

The Book of books in its 3,500 year history has defied the ravages of time and survived thousands of copyings and translations. Empires have risen and fallen, thousands of wars have been fought, plagues and natural disasters have swept the earth, and throughout all the Bible has been preserved for past, present, and future generations.

Many of the acts of God, human events, and conversations recorded in the Bible were written down hundreds of years after they happened. There was no on-the-scene reporter to document the first five "days" or stages of creation. It is also doubtful that the stories of the quarrel between Cain and Abel, the fall of the Tower of Babel, and the Flood were written down when they occurred. These stories were probably passed along from generation to generation before finally being recorded by the inspired historian, Moses.

The Old Testament, except for a few Aramaic passages (Ezra 4:8-6:18; 7:12-26; Jeremiah 10: 11; and Daniel 2:4-7:28), was written in Hebrew. The Hebrew language was originally written entirely in consonants and without spacing between the words. Genesis 1: would appear thus (if it were English):

NTHBGNNNGGDCRTDTHHVNNDTHRTH

Not until after the return of the Jews from Babylonian captivity were words divided from one another and generally arranged into paragraphs. Such changes were only gradually introduced by the scribes, beginning about the time of Ezra. Vowels were inserted even later, about A.D. 500 to 800, by the Masoretes who produced the Masoretic Hebrew Old Testament.

Difficulty in the copying of ancient manuscripts

also arises from the fact that many of the Hebrew consonant characters are similar, and they almost beg for copying mistakes to be made. For example: R equals ר ; DH equals ד ; and W equals ו . H ה and T ת are similar, and so are N נ and G ג . However, Hebrew copyists were reverently and meticulously accurate in their work. Every letter was counted. When the copying was finished, the scribe counted the letters in his copy. If the two totals did not agree, a search was made for the errors. The Hebrew Bible was literally reproduced jot by jot, tittle by tittle, dot by dot.

Various Writing Materials Used

All sorts of materials were used by the ancients for writing—stone, leaves, bark, wood, metals, baked clay, and so on. The Hebrew Scriptures were mainly transmitted on specially prepared animal skins called vellum or parchment. Hebrew Talmudic law specified that all copies of the Law used in public worship should be inscribed on skins of clean animals and in roll form. Modern Hebrews still use similar rolls in public worship. Many ancient leather rolls used by the Hebrews are now in museums and libraries.

The original manuscripts of the Hebrew Old Testament are assumed to have been worn out long ago. Also, when a scroll was recopied, the deteriorating scroll from which the copy was made was usually destroyed. In 1947, however, the entire book of Isaiah, excepting two small parts, was discovered in a cave northwest of the Dead Sea. The parchment had been hidden in an earthenware jar, wrapped in yards of cloth, and covered with pitch. Experts believe this copy was written during the first century B.C.—about 1,000 years before the oldest previously known Hebrew manuscript of a book of the Bible. The Dead Sea Scrolls were undoubtedly in use while Christ was on earth. A few Hebrew manuscripts discovered since 1947 may be even older.

Writing was more advanced in the first century during which the 27 books of the New Testament are believed to have been written. That we do not have original manuscripts for the New Testament books is accounted for by the fact that the papyrus writing materials used in the first century world lacked one very important quality—durability.

Papyrus paper came from the pith of the papyrus plant which was cut into thin strips, laid down in a crosspatch, glued, pressed, and dried to form sheets. The sheets were fastened together to make a roll up to 35 feet long—enough to contain the Gospel of Matthew.

Scholars generally assume that the New Testament originals were written on scrolls of papyrus paper; the use of scrolls was customary in Old Testament books and important literary works. Many of the New Testament manuscripts, however, were written in codex form (like a book). The originals, or "autographs," crumbled as the paper became brittle with age. All copies of the Scriptures and other papyrus literature made outside of Egypt during the first century are assumed to have perished.

Each Book a Separate Manuscript

Each New Testament book at first was a writing by itself and circulated in the area to which it was written. For example, some scholars think the Gospel of Matthew was written for Palestinian and Syrian Christians and circulated within the Antioch church while the Book of Mark was written especially for the Christians at Rome and circulated there. The Gospel of Luke circulated among the churches of Greece; and the Book of John was read by Christians in Ephesus. Then as the other New Testament books were written, churches exchanged Gospels and Epistles.

About 144 to 150 A.D. a controversial churchman named Marcion collected ten of Paul's epistles and the Gospel of Luke and listed them as a canon of sacred writings. Marcion, however, took the liberty of striking out a few verses and phrases that didn't fit his peculiar ideas about God and the Old Testament. Marcion and his followers formed a separate church that existed into the fifth century.

Marcion is credited with making the first attempt to list a canon of New Testament Scriptures. The New Testament canon grew as other books were added to those selected by Marcion. By about 350 A.D. the New Testament canon as we have it today was complete. In 367 A.D. the noted theologian Athanasius, leader of the Christians in Alexandria, Egypt, said, concerning the New Testament canon, "In these alone is the teaching of godliness heralded. Let no one add to these. Let nothing be taken away."

The New Testament Canon

There was no single body of churchmen to pronounce the canon "official." No one had the authority to lay down qualifying rules to determine which books were to be a part of the canon. But by divine providence and selection by many widely scattered churches, the New Testament came to be in its present form—a collection of books believed to be the writings of apostles or their immediate disciples. Apostolic authorship was a major factor in determining if a book was "inspired."

Many religious writings were judged unacceptable and were not included in the canon of inspired writings. The "Acts of John" told of John miraculously driving all the bedbugs out of his bed, and the "Acts of Thomas" included the story of a dragon punished for squirting poison on an enemy. The "Acts of Paul" told of Paul baptizing a lion. The "Acts of Peter" mentioned a dry sardine that was made to swim again. The Christians apparently felt that such fairy tales were uninspired and these spurious books were recognized as unauthentic from the time of their first appearance. Early Christians also rejected some better books. Tatian's "Harmony of the Four Gospels" was widely read but not included as a canonical book; perhaps because the four Gospels were available already, or it may have been because the compiler was not an apostle.

The early churches added the New Testament canon of 27 books to the 39 Old Testament books already accepted as inspired to make the complete Bible as it now is. Fifteen more books (today called "The Apocrypha"), written chiefly between the time of Malachi and John the Baptist, were not canonized by the early Christians for a good reason: These books were not accepted by the Jews as inspired Scripture. Not until the Council of Trent in 1546 did the Roman Catholic Church finally and officially insert most of the Apocrypha into the Catholic Bible.

Early Manuscripts and Fragments

The earliest major manuscripts of the larger

parts of the Bible are *Codex Sinaiticus*, mentioned earlier, and *Codex Vaticanus*, now in the Vatican. These were probably written in the fourth century and contain almost all of both Testaments.

Papyrus fragments exist in Greek that are older than *Codex Sinaiticus* and *Codex Vaticanus*; the oldest is probably *Rylands Papyrus*, found in Egypt in 1920 and now in the John Rylands Library in Manchester, England. It measures 3½ by 2½ inches and contains John 18:31-33, 37, 38. Scholars assign the writing of this manuscript to about 150 A.D., less than 50 years after the death of the apostle John.

Numerous quotations from the New Testament are found in the writings of the early church fathers who lived in the second and third centuries. Years ago a group of English scholars debated the question: Suppose every copy of the New Testament had been destroyed by the end of the third century, could enough be compiled from the writings of the fathers to reconstruct the text? Two months later, Sir David Dalrymple showed the scholars a pile of books and said, "I've read all the existing works of the second and third century fathers and have found the entire New Testament except eleven verses."

Actually thousands of old manuscripts are available to testify to the accuracy of the New Testament text. One scholar has counted 4,105 Greek manuscripts of portions of the New Testament. Over 15,000 Latin versions plus 1,000 other early versions of the New Testament are in existence. In contrast, only one manuscript preserves the records of the historian Tacitus, and only a few manuscripts exist of the writings of such thinkers as Sophocles, Virgil, and Cicero. No other ancient book possesses as much manuscript evidence as does the Bible.

The first great translator of the entire Bible was Jerome. The Old Testament had been translated into the *Greek Septuagint* beginning about 285 B.C. Jerome began work in Rome, then moved to the Holy Land. Driven by criticism, he continued his work in a cave near Bethlehem. Completed in 405 A.D., Jerome's Latin translation made use of earlier Latin translations and Hebrew and Greek manuscripts. In 1546 Jerome's *Latin Vulgate* was proclaimed the only authentic and authorized translation of the Catholic Church. In 1592 Pope Clement VIII forbade any additional change in the text.

The Beginning of Translations

During the Dark Ages the Scriptures, for the most part, remained locked in the Hebrew, Greek, and Latin languages. The Bible was not generally available to the common people. One exception was a translation of the Gospel of John by the

Venerable Bede completed shortly before his death in the eighth century. Another exception came shortly before 900 A.D. when King Alfred the Great ordered the translation of the whole Bible into Anglo-Saxon. The translation of the whole Bible was not completed during this time, however. Little more was done until the time of Wycliffe, over four centuries later.

It is often said that about 1250, Cardinal Hugo divided the Bible into chapters; but some attribute this to Stephen Langton. Verse divisions in the New Testament were made in 1551 by Robert Stephanus. One story tells that he worked while riding horseback. This is said to account for the unnatural verse divisions in some places.

John Wycliffe, born about 1320, translated the Bible into the English language. His main source of reference in translation work was Jerome's *Latin Vulgate*. Each Wycliffe Bible took about ten months to write by hand and cost over $200. Those who could not afford to buy it, would pay to read it one hour a day. Sometimes a farmer would exchange a load of hay for a few pages of the precious Book.

Wycliffe was fiercely opposed by church leaders. Forty years after his death his bones were ordered dug up, burned, and cast into a stream. The ashes flowed away to the ocean, symbolizing the spread of his translation to other lands.

John Huss read Wycliffe's works and prepared a translation of the Bible in the language of Bohemia (now Czechoslovakia). A century later, Martin Luther meditated upon the Latin Scriptures and proclaimed, "No Christian can be compelled to hold any doctrine not contained in Holy Scriptures." Calvin, Zwingli, Knox, and other reformers studied the Scriptures and the mighty Reformation began that resulted in the great Protestant denominations we know today.

As the Reformers were crying, "Back to the Bible," a discovery of far-reaching importance was made. About A.D. 1450 Johann Gutenberg designed and built a printing press and printed a Bible. (A copy of Gutenberg's first printed Bible is now in the Library of Congress and is valued at over $1,000,000.) Copies of the Bible then became available to the masses for the first time in history.

Shortly after Gutenberg cranked the first Bible off his press, Erasmus, a learned Greek scholar, produced a Greek New Testament from Greek manuscripts.

English Translations Appear

In 1525 William Tyndale made an English translation from Erasmus' New Testament. Church leaders rewarded Tyndale by burning him at the stake in 1536.

A year after Tyndale's death, Miles Coverdale translated the first complete English Bible.

Persecution eased about the time Coverdale's translation appeared, and one English Bible translation after another followed in rapid succession. In the haste to get the Bible to the masses who could not read Latin, Greek, or Hebrew, many errors were made. One translation had Psalm 119: 161 read, "Printers have persecuted me without a cause." Another problem was the rapid changing of the English language and its word definitions. This caused problems for translators and readers alike. The *Taverner Bible* recorded a messenger reporting to King David during a battle as saying, "I saw a great hurlee burlee" (11 Samuel 18: 29).

The *Great Bible,* named for its size (13¾ × 9½ inches), was published in 1539. Thomas Cromwell, the King's chief minister, ordered copies set up in every church. Seven editions were printed between 1539-41 and they had enormous influence on the English populace. Each Bible had a congregation of readers.

The *King James Bible,* however, outstripped the Great Bible in influence. It was based upon the best current Greek translations and manuscripts then available and was published by order of King James I in 1611. The King James version of the Bible is still the best selling of all Bible translations.

The repulsive character of James I serves to accent the sovereignty of God in using unworthy men to promote the Scriptures. Historian J. R. Green wrote of this monarch, "His big head, his slobbering tongue, his quilted clothes, his rickety legs, his goggle eyes, stood out as a grotesque contrast with all that men recalled of Henry and Elizabeth as did his gaffle and rodomontade, his want of personal dignity, his coarse buffoonery, his drunkenness, his pedantry, his contemptible cowardice."

The oldest Greek manuscripts used by King James' scholars dated back to the tenth century A.D. In the following years scholars searched laboriously for older manuscripts. Some made great personal sacrifices to seek out the purest text. The English scholar Tregelles, for example, went blind while deciphering ancient documents. Other scholars combed old monasteries and dug in old ruins in search of precious manuscripts.

Ancient Parchments Are Found

Tischendorf, a German professor, traveled to Bible lands and in 1844 came to a monastery at the foot of Mt. Sinai. In the monastery he found a basket full of old parchments used for starting fires. The parchment leaves were the most ancient manuscripts he had ever seen. By much effort he persuaded the monks to give him the treasure, which was eventually delivered to the Russian Imperial Library at St. Petersburg. This was the *Codex Siniaticus,* previously mentioned, that was purchased by the British government in 1933 for a half million dollars.

Tischendorf's manuscript contains the Greek New Testament written about 350 A.D.—almost seven centuries earlier than the oldest source manuscript used in preparing the *King James Bible.*

In 1881 the Revised New Testament was published—a revision made from the best manuscript evidence available by leading Biblical scholars in England and America. Every word from the beginning of Matthew to the end of Romans—118,000 words—was telegraphed from New York to Chicago. This may be the longest telegraphic message ever sent!

Other revisions of the Bible have since been published. English readers may now select from about a score of different translations.

In making major translations and revisions, scholars study the best and oldest manuscripts, paying careful attention to points of difference. The marvel is that the thousands of old manuscripts differ so little. The late Dr. A. T. Robertson estimated that between the oldest known manuscripts and the King James text there is conflict in only one thousandth of the entire text, and in no case is a major Christian doctrine affected.

Worldwide Bible Societies

Bible translation and publication continues at a fast pace. The leading Bible publisher today is the American Bible Society established in 1816. The American Bible Society and 26 other national societies now cooperate in the United Bible Societies that operate around the world.

The leading translation agency is the Wycliffe Bible Translators and its sister organization, the Summer Institute of Linguistics. Wycliffe has about 2,400 translators and support personnel (ranging from jungle pilots to expert typists now serving in 19 countries and translating into 420 different languages for as many tribal peoples. Wycliffe translators have penetrated some of the most remote and primitive areas of the world in New Guinea, the Amazon jungle, Vietnam, Surinam, and other places.

Many Wycliffe translations are published by the American Bible Society. Both agencies consider themselves servants of all denominations and spread the Scriptures on a non-sectarian basis.*

* For more information on these organizations, write to the American Bible Society at 450 Park Avenue, New York, N.Y. 10022, and the Wycliffe Bible Translators at Box 1960, Santa Ana, California 92702.

Wycliffe, for example has provided linguistic training for over 15,000 missionary candidates from 125 mission boards.

As of 1968, one book or more of the Bible has been published in 1,337 different languages and dialects. Former headhunters in New Guinea and Amazonia are now reading, for the first time, the Scriptures in their own languages.

New languages are being added at the rate of about one a month. Wycliffe's General Director, W. Cameron Townsend, estimates there are still 2,000 tongues, spoken by 150 million Bibleless tribesmen. Wycliffe has announced a goal to decipher and translate Scripture into all of these languages by the year 2000.

Not until every man has the Bible in his native tongue will the work of translation be completed. Even then a vast task of literacy education will still challenge the Church.

For 3,500 years the Bible has moved along the highway of history and among the babel of tongues, proclaiming God's message to people of every race and nation. That the inspired Word has been transported and transmitted so accurately is indeed a wonder.

CHAPTER 3

IT TRIUMPHS TESTS OF TIME

History has proven the Bible to be like the Irishman's wall which was built four feet wide and three feet high. When asked why he had been so foolish as to build a wall wider than it was high, the Irishman replied, "I built it so if a storm should come and blow it over, it will be higher afterwards than it was before."

No book has weathered so many storms and survived as has the Bible. Emperors and kings, power-hungry churchmen, and infidel scholars have howled and raged against the Bible. In both ancient and modern times mobs have burned the Bible in public squares, and soldiers have ransacked homes to find and destroy the Book of eternity. All opposition has proven futile. Like the Irishman's wall, the Bible comes back higher than before in influence and power. Indeed, the enemies of the Bible always suffer the fate predicted in the prophecy of Jeremiah: "Is not my word like as a fire? saith the Lord; and like a hammer that breaketh the rock in pieces?" (Jeremiah 23: 29).

Enemies sought to destroy the Bible even before all 66 books were written. King Manasseh of Judah

46

(697-642 B.C.) encouraged all forms of paganism —even the sacrifice of children to Molech—and very likely destroyed all copies of the Law that he could find. Yet 20 years after his death, Manasseh's grandson, Josiah, found the lost book of the Law in the Temple and called for public reading and observance of the Law. A mighty religious revival resulted.

Bible Owners Persecuted

About 500 years later—during the inter-Testamental period—the Syrian despot, Antiochus Epiphanes, gained control of Palestine. He plundered the Temple at Jerusalem, sacrificed swine on the altar, and destroyed all the Old Testament books he could find. His soldiers killed and tortured hundreds of Jews. Anyone found possessing a copy of the Hebrew Scriptures was condemned to death on the spot. Antiochus appointed inspectors to see that the Scriptures were neither read nor observed and that the people offered sacrifices to pagan gods.

Many courageous Jews defied the Syrian King and paid with their lives. One youth told Antiochus to his face, "I obey only the command of the Law that was given to our forefathers through Moses." He was immediately slaughtered.

The massacres, Bible burnings, and plunder of the Temple caused a revolt. An old priest named

Mattathias fled to the hills with his sons, called the Maccabees, and began a rebellion that resulted in defeat of the foreign invaders. Three years after Antiochus had ordered the Hebrew Scriptures destroyed, the despot died in disgrace. According to I Maccabees 6: 12, 13 (one of the books of the *Apocrypha*) he said as he was dying, "Now I remember the wrongs which I did in Jerusalem . . . it is because of this that these misfortunes have overtaken me."

Back in Jerusalem, the Temple was soon repaired, worship reinstituted, and the Scriptures again taught to the people.

After the Romans took control of Palestine, they hesitated to interfere with Jewish religious customs. They allowed the Scriptures to circulate and be read and taught. At first they even ignored the Christian movement, thinking it was only a sect of the Jews. But after a time, numerous clashes began over the issue of whether Christ or Caesar was supreme Lord.

Christians Murdered in Gaul

Many Christians were murdered when they refused to worship the emperor. The aged Polycarp, disciple of the apostle John, was one of many burned at the stake. Around 177 A.D. swarms of Christians were murdered in Gaul, their bodies burned, and the ashes thrown into the Rhone

Hebrew scroll, probably transcribed about the 15th century A.D. The writing is from left to right, and there are no vowels.

Johann Gutenberg printed the first Bible from movable type. The Congressional Library purchased one of three known copies for over $300,000 (Picture is from the film, *Our Bible, How it Came to Us*).

I

American Bible Society Photo

The Great Bible, named because of its size, was one of many English Bibles printed following the development of movable type. This copy was printed in 1562.

A Bible translator uses a tape recorder as a tool for analyzing the Duna language of New Guinea.

Wycliffe Bible Translators Photo

An Auca literacy class in Ecuador is learning to read the
Gospels in the Auca language.

A translator in Mexico selected
this bright young man as his
language helper; the two may
work together for years.

In Peru, this Piro Indian boy ex-
changes a treasured tiger skin for a
New Testament he will treasure even
more.

III

A Bible launch distributes Bibles on one of the thousands of water highways in Southeast Asia.

Processing translations for printing has been reduced from years to weeks by computers and automatic typesetters.

The American Bible Society has distributed more than 900,000,000 copies of the Scriptures since its founding in 1816. Early in this century, Bibles sold for 17¢ a copy. Bible salesmen are called *colporteurs,* from a French word meaning "to peddle."

American Bible Society Photo

A *colporteur* in India explains Bible passages in the Tamil language. He is using a literacy chart to help the man learn to read the Bible for himself.

Chief Tariri of Amazonia killed ten chiefs plus an uncounted number of common jungle Indians before two women Bible translators introduced him to the Word of God. Since becoming a Christian, Chief Tariri has renounced his murderous ways and is now a missionary to former enemies.

Wycliffe Bible Translators Photo

On a lake shore in Mexico a *colporteur* tells friendly fishermen the story of the Fisher of men and offers them portions and selections of the Scriptures printed in Spanish.

Former President Dwight D. Eisenhower received the 500,000,001st volume of Scripture printed by the American Bible Society since its inception in 1816.

Another former president, Harry S. Truman, accepted a presentation of various Bibles for the Truman Library in Independence, Mo.

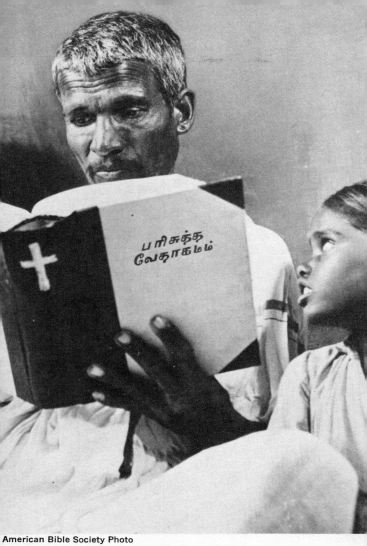

A father reads to his son in a village in South India.

Printed in U.S.A.

River. Bishop Pothinus was tortured and Attalus, his keeper, burned to death on a chair of red hot iron.

By the dawn of the third century, churches were flourishing all over the empire. Confiscation of property, loss of jobs, imprisonment, torture, and even death had not dimmed the torch of faith held by millions.

Emperor Diocletian became aware that the Christians gained renewed strength and courage from reading the Jewish prophets and the new Christian writings in their worship services. In the year 303 he began a savage persecution. He decreed the destruction of church properties all over the empire and the burning of all Scriptures.

Thousands of Christians perished, but within a decade, Diocletian was dead, perhaps by his own hand.

In 313 the new co-rulers of the empire, Licinius of the East and Constantine of the West, declared full toleration for Christianity. The Emperor Constantine became a professed Christian himself, won sole authority in a power struggle, and encouraged every person in the empire to read the Christian Scriptures. Like the Irishman's wall, the Bible had again come back taller than before the storm.

Christianity prospered and the Scriptures were circulated in every corner of the empire. The canon of 27 New Testament books plus the Jewish Old Testament became almost universally recognized.

Clergy Oppose Bible Reading

The church grew and solidified into a monarchy with central power held by the bishop of Rome. As the Rome-ruled church grew in number and influence, a more dangerous threat to the Bible appeared—clerical opposition.

Three centuries before Martin Luther, the Waldensians were excommunicated by Pope Lucius III and became the forerunners of future Protestantism. They were simple, spiritual people who kept the Bible central in their worship. Catholic authorities became fearful that the Waldensian church would grow if the Bible became open to the masses. During the preceding "Dark Ages," few Bibles existed and these were mainly studied in monasteries. In 1229, a Catholic synod in Toulouse, France, forbade the laity to possess the Scriptures, except the Psalms and a few verses contained in prayer books. The synod especially denounced all Bible translations.

Other church authorities followed suit, especially in Spain. However, there was never universal denial of Bible reading during the Middle Ages.

Reformers who promoted Bible reading paid with their lives. One was John Huss, the pastor of Prague, who proclaimed, "The Bible, not the church, is the Christian's sole authority." First Huss' Bibles and books were burned, then he was burned alive by order of a church council.

Martin Luther Read the Bible

Martin Luther, living a century later, discovered his first whole Bible in a university library. His Biblical studies led him into direct conflict with the established church. His famous stand before the German emperor's assembly at Worms ("Unless I am refuted by Scripture, or clear reason . . . my conscience is bound to the Word of God. I cannot and I will not recant anything, for to go against conscience is neither right nor safe. Here I stand; I cannot do otherwise. God help me.") led to his being declared an outlaw. Luther had to hide, but while in hiding he translated the New Testament into the German language. Five thousand copies were snapped up in less than three months.

As spearheads of the Reformation advanced across Europe, the Roman church took a harder line against lay possession and reading of the Bible.* Some state monarchs, notably "Bloody"

* Many modern Catholic leaders—notably the late Pope John XXIII—have promoted Bible reading. Father Louis Hartman, Bible scholar and Secretary of the Catholic Biblical Association, told the author, "Bible study is being pushed. Many parishes have Bible study groups in which a lay group meets to read a section of the Bible and discuss it."

Queen Mary of England, ordered Bible printing and distribution stopped at the price of blood.

Benjamin Franklin wrote of his great-great-grandfather fastening a Bible under a stool. When he wanted to read to the family, he simply turned the stool upside down. As he read, one of the children stood at the door to watch for "Bloody" Mary's soldiers.

Queen Mary's five-year reign of terror finally ended with her death in 1558. Her half-sister Elizabeth came to the throne and quickly reversed royal policy toward the Bible.

Queen Elizabeth Prints 130 Editions

Queen Elizabeth ordered a Bible placed in every court office and called the Bible "the jewel I love best." Ninety editions of the *Geneva Version* were published during her long reign plus 40 editions of other versions. For the first time, the Bible became a best seller.

The Reformation that had produced the great Protestant denominations gave the Bible to the masses. Neither church nor state rulers had been able to keep the Bible locked away in musty monasteries and bishops' palaces. The Bible, however, was not destined to be free from future attack. A new foe arose that championed religious freedom but denied the authority of the Bible in the name of scholarship.

Voltaire (1694-1778), the noted French scholar, scorned the Bible. Yet after his death, the printing press which had printed his attacks on the Bible was used to print copies of the Bible. The very house in which he had lived became a Bible house for the Geneva Bible Society.

In the next century, Ernest Renan (1823-1892) led the attacks against the Bible and the divinity of Christ. However, the brilliant Renan turned to the Bible for guidance in his closing years and left this testimony:

"O man of Galilee, Thou hast conquered. Henceforth no man shall distinguish between Thee and God!"

The twentieth century brought fresh attacks upon the Bible by dictators and godless nations. In 1939 the Russians attacked Finland and destroyed the Bible House of the Finnish church and their stock of Bibles. The British and Foreign Bible Society came to the rescue and in 1940, 243,000 volumes of Scripture were distributed in Finland.

Hitler set out to exterminate the Jews, strangle the Christian faith, and make *Mein Kampf* the Bible of a "Master Race" and himself the savior. Now Hitler has perished, and dedicated German missionaries are going to primitive countries to translate the Bible.

Emperor Hirohito of Japan joined Hitler in attempting world conquest. Japanese militarists encouraged the people to worship Hirohito as a god. Now Hirohito's myth of deity has been demolished. He is no longer the object of mass worship. Thousands of Bibles are being distributed in Japan to schools and libraries. Captain Mitsuo Fuchida, the Japanese pilot who led the attack on Pearl Harbor, has become a preacher of the Bible.

Communism—Modern Bible Foe

Now Communism has come to dwarf all other foes of the Bible. Missionaries have been banished from Russia, China, and other Communist countries. Churches have been closed. Sunday schools are not allowed. Presses that once printed Bibles now print atheistic propaganda. Yet many people are reported to still have Bibles. Christian broadcasters have received letters from behind the Iron and Bamboo Curtains that indicate faith is very much alive.

The story of Nikolai Alexandrenko is only one illustration of how the Bible can triumph over Communism. Alexandrenko grew up in Russia and was taught that the Bible is a book of myths. While fighting in the Russian army, he was captured by the Germans and taken to a concentration camp. After World War II ended, he found two Bible verses on a scrap of paper. This led to his conversion and training in a theological seminary. Today he teaches the Bible to young ministers in a Baptist college.

Evidence of a new method of attack upon the Bible has been discovered in North Korea. Bibles have been discovered with cleverly inserted bits of Communist propaganda. We may be assured that this, too, will fail. Long after Communism becomes a musty ideology of history, the Bible will still be read in its purest form.

American magazines have recently been filled with declarations of certain Protestant "theologians" who not only reduce the Bible to a collection of myths, but say very loudly that God is dead. They—and others not so radical—are beating the drums for a so-called "intelligent religion." They deny the supernatural, and respect only those portions of the Bible which appeal to radicals. These attacks, too, will fail. Again, we need not fear. The Bible—like the Irishman's wall—will still be standing long after the "Christian atheists" have been stilled by death.

John Clifford has given us an accurate poetic description of what has happened to the enemies of the Bible.

Last eve I paused beside the blacksmith's door
And heard the anvil ring the vesper chimes;
Then looking in, I saw upon the floor
Old hammers worn out with beating years of time.

"How many anvils have you had," said I,
"To wear and batter all these hammers so?"
"Just one," said he and then with twinkling eye,
"The anvil wears the hammers out, you know."

And so I thought, the anvil of God's Word
For ages skeptics' blows have beat upon,
Yet, though the noise of falling blows was heard,
The anvil is unharmed, the hammers are gone.

"But the word of the Lord endureth forever" (I Peter 1: 25a).

John Jewell said, "Cities fall, empires come to nothing, kingdoms fade away as smoke. Where is Numa, Minos, Lycurgus? Where are their books? and what has become of their laws? But that this Book no tyrant should have been able to consume, no tradition to choke, no heretic maliciously to corrupt; that it should stand unto this day, amid the wreck of all that was human, without the alteration of one sentence so as to change the doctrine taught therein,—surely there is a very singular providence, claiming our attention in a most remarkable manner."

CHAPTER 4

IT INFLUENCES DECISIONS THAT DECIDE DESTINY

The Bible is like tritium, a chemical tracer used in scientific detective work. Tritium can be diluted a million, million, million times—and still be detected!

Oil producers use tritium to follow the flow of oil through the pore spaces of rock hundreds of feet underground. The tracer is put into a central input well where it mixes with the natural petroleum material. Gas is then pumped into the central well to push the petroleum through the rock and out into the producing wells. Chemical analysis of oil from the producing wells reveals the presence of the tritium tracer and assures the producers that petroleum is flowing from the input well.

Likewise, the influence of the Bible is detectable in all areas and levels of human society. Examine social advances, education, government, commerce, literature, arts, and science, and you will find the Bible a respected authority. No book has cast so great a shadow of influence for good upon the world scene as has the Bible.

Sir Francis Bacon said, "There never was found, in any age of the world, either religion or law that did so highly exalt the public good as the Bible."

The naming of children shows the influence of the Bible. Under Teutonic rule, children in England were given such names as Aelfric, Caedmon, and Cynewulf, but because of the influence of the Bible, by 1300 one Englishman of every five was named in honor of the apostle John. Today, millions of people bear such Biblical names as John, Peter, Moses, Adam, James, Thomas, Paul, Mary, Joseph, Martha, Elizabeth, Philip, and Stephen.

The influence of the Bible upon humanity, however, has gone far beyond names. Families and persons have been given value and dignity largely unknown before the Bible was circulated beyond the borders of Palestine.

This description of the early Christians was written in the ancient *Epistle to Diognetus*:

"They marry as do all; they beget children; but they do not commit abortion. They have a common table but not a common bed. They are in the flesh, but they do not live after the flesh. They pass their days on earth, but they are citizens of heaven. They obey the prescribed laws, and . . .

surpass the laws by their lives. They love all men, and are persecuted by all."

The Bible produced the idea of human equality and brotherhood. It aroused Christians to free their slaves and feed the poor and needy. Clement of Lactantius, an early church leader, declared, "In God's sight no one is a slave, no one a master, for if all have the same father, by an equal right we are all children."

Bible Teaching on Marriage

The Bible teaches that marriage is the union of one man and one woman and can only be dissolved for the cause of adultery. Thus, polygamy and concubinage have disappeared from the lands where the Bible is widely studied. The increase of divorce, notably in the United States, is not the result of Biblical teaching, but in spite of it.

Hinduism classifies women with cows, mares, female camels, and goats. "A cow," so goes a Hindu proverb, "is sanctified, but a woman is depraved." The Bible has lifted women from the roles of animals, playthings, and servants of men to a position of dignity.

Before Biblical views spread throughout the Roman world, Roman fathers held the right of life and death over their children. Infanticide and exposure of children was then widely practiced and still is in non-Christian areas of the world.

Plato and Aristotle agreed that children should be abandoned when parents were unable to rear them or if because of weakness or deformity they showed no promise of service to the state. Seneca wrote: "Monstrous offspring we destroy; children, too, if weak and unnaturally formed at birth, we drown. It is not anger, but reason, thus to separate the useless from the sound." A saying of the ancient world was: "A man is a wolf to those he does not know."

When Christianity became the religion of the Roman Empire, the Emperor Constantine decreed in 315 A.D. that parents must not kill their new-born children and that if they could not support them, government revenues must be used.

The first orphanages were operated by Christian widows and deaconesses under the direction of pastors. The first charity hospital of record was founded outside the walls of Rome in 380 A.D. by Fabiola, a devout Christian. Other refuges for unfortunates were established soon afterwards. Thalasius, a Christian monk, founded a home for blind beggars on the banks of the Euphrates River. St. Basil founded the first hospitals in Asia. St. Chrysostom built other hospitals in Constantinople. The first asylums for the insane were opened in Spain under Christian auspices. By aiding those whom the pagans forsook, the Christians were heeding the words of Christ, "Inasmuch as ye have done it unto one of the least of these my brethren, ye have done it unto me" (Matthew 25: 40).

The Bible and Social Reform

During the Dark Ages, when the Bible was not generally taught, the social reforms were all but wiped out. A resurgence of social action came with the Protestant Reformation and the translation of the Bible into the languages of the people. Open Bibles opened hearts to the needs of mankind.

Florence Nightingale, a devout Bible believer, transformed hospital care and pioneered the nursing profession for women. John Howard, the sheriff of Bedfordshire, England, in 1773 began reforms in prison practices. He found prisoners branded, brutally beaten, their ears cropped. Many were imprisoned because of debt and were kept there until the last farthing was paid. Howard's Christian ideals were revealed in a prayer just before his death, "O Lord, visit the prisoners and captives and manifest thy strength in my weakness."

At about the same time, newspaper publisher Robert Raikes led a campaign to reclaim the wild children that ran like rats through the streets of England's cities. Raikes' reforms led to the establishment of the Sunday school that has spread the teachings of the Bible to every corner of the earth.

A few years later, Elizabeth Fry marched on

London's Newgate Prison and found women and babies jammed into a dungeon like wild animals. She and other Quaker ladies taught the prisoners the Bible and the three "R's," and pressured the politicians to begin reforms.

Across the Atlantic another "angel of mercy" went to teach the Bible to the women prisoners in East Cambridge, Massachusetts. She could hardly hear herself for the wild screams coming from another part of the jail. Investigation disclosed that the disturbers were, in the words of the jailer, "two screeching lunatics who ought to be gagged." More investigation convinced Dorothea Dix that the mentally ill should be released from dungeons and hospitalized. With Bible in hand, the thin, frail school teacher demanded that state legislatures transfer to hospitals the innocent ones "locked in cages, closets, cellars, stalls, and pens; chained, naked, beaten with rods, and lashed into obedience." Reforms followed in America, Canada, Scotland, England, and Italy.

Less well known is the story of how reindeer came to the Alaskan Eskimos. Missionary Sheldon Jackson personally brought the first reindeer from Siberia to Alaska by ship in 1891 and saved thousands of Alaskan Eskimos from starvation.

History is filled with other examples of mercy projects and institutions that were inspired by the teaching of the Bible. Wherever the Bible has gone, even among the most primitive tribes, mercy and moral reforms have followed.

Biblical Influence on Education

The Bible has had an immeasurable influence on schools and education. The Jews obeyed Biblical commands and taught their children in homes and synagogues. Christian primary schools are known to have existed in the fourth century A.D. The church Council of Chalon, in 813, decreed that church leaders should establish schools for teaching Scripture and literature. About the twelfth century, the forerunners of the present great European universities began appearing with their main objective to teach the Bible and theology. The greatest scientists of pre- and post-reformation times were students of the Bible—Galileo, Faraday, Pascal, Newton and others.

The Protestant Reformation gave impetus to the Biblical idea that every person is directly responsible to God for his conduct, with the conclusion following that everyone must be informed by education. Thus, in future years came free public education.

The first American schools were founded primarily to teach the Bible. Apart from state chartered colleges and universities, almost every college and university has been founded by some branch of the Christian church.

Harvard University was founded in 1636 by Reverend John Harvard to train young men for the ministry. Yale (1701) and Princeton (1747) were founded partly for the same purpose. William and Mary College in Virginia was established "that the church in Virginia may be furnished with . . . ministers of the Gospel, and that the youth may be piously educated in good manners and that the Christian faith may be propagated amongst the western Indians to the glory of Almighty God."

The University of Pennsylvania, Dartmouth College, and Brown University are three of many now-famous schools of learning that came as a result of the Biblical revival led by George Whitefield.

The first of the state institutions, a model for all the rest, the University of Michigan, was established through the joint efforts of four clergymen.

Two great Bible-based organizations are now advancing education into primitive, underdeveloped areas of the world. The already mentioned Wycliffe Bible Translators learn and write down previously unwritten languages, translate the Scriptures, help prepare primers in the tribal languages, and aid national educators in training native teachers.

Thousands of simplified readers for new literates, based on the Gospels and called "The Story of Jesus," have been printed by the David C. Cook Foundation and other publishers and distributed by the Laubach organization. Laubach Literacy Inc. is welcomed in over 100 countries and is credited with teaching 300 million illiterates to read.

And still the story of the Bible's influence is not complete.

The Bible and Government

Consider government: By obeying the instructions of the "Books of the Law," the Jews advanced from a disorganized mob of slaves to become, under Solomon, the most glorious nation of the world. Israel's power waned only when the nation ceased to obey God's words in Scripture.

The early Christians were first ignored, then persecuted, and finally elevated to leadership in the Roman Empire. Had not the Emperor Constantine adopted Bible-inspired reforms, the Empire would probably have fallen a century earlier than it did.

In more recent centuries, numerous nations have risen and fallen according to their acceptance or rejection of the Bible. Consider only England and the United States.

The three greatest periods of English history came when national recognition was given to the Bible as God's Word:

—During the reign of Alfred the Great, who took a personal interest in having parts of the Bible

translated, England rose from barbarism, division, and ignorance into a united, civilized nation.
—During the reign of Queen Elizabeth (who first officially promoted the circulation of the Bible), England became a world power for the first time.
—During the reign of Queen Victoria, the British Empire climbed to its zenith in world influence. When asked by a foreign prince the secret of her country's greatness, Victoria replied, "The Bible, my lord."

Early immigrants came to the New World seeking freedom to interpret the Bible for themselves. The Bible was the textbook of early America not only in schools, but in the highest circles of government. Our fundamental freedoms were based upon the Bible.

Puritan Bible scholars founded the colonies and molded the moral concepts of the infant democracy. Other than the Bible, the best-read book in the colonies was the *New England Primer* which could better be called the *Bible Primer*. Under the letter A was:

> *"In Adam's fall*
> *We sinned all."*

And under Z:

> *"Zacchaeus, he*
> *Did climb a tree*
> *Our Lord to see."*

Noah Webster, of dictionary fame, began his famous blue-backed *Speller* with this prayer:

> *"No man may put off the law of God.*
> *My joy is in His law all the day.*
> *O may I not go in the way of sin.*
> *Let me not go in the way of ill men."*

His famous *American Dictionary*, on which he toiled for over 20 years, was filled with definitions that alluded to the Bible and its teachings. Some examples:

Love: The Christian *loves* his Bible. If our hearts are right, we *love* God above all things.

Knowledge: God has a perfect *knowledge* of all His works. Human *knowledge* is very limited.

Hope: A well founded Scriptural *hope,* is, in our religion, the source of ineffable happiness.

In his 77th year Webster wrote his daughter Harriet, "The longer I live, the stronger is my faith in the truth of the Scriptures." He spent the closing years of his life trying to up-date the language of the King James Bible.

One of the earliest acts of Congress was to approve the printing of a large edition of the Bible and officially recommend that every citizen read therefrom. George Washington took his oath of office with his hand on the Bible, as has every President since. While not all of the architects of

American democracy were Christians, *all* were students of the Bible. Their writings were filled with Biblical quotations.

Statements by four Presidents reflect America's traditional respect for the Bible:

—George Washington: "It is impossible to rightly govern the world without God and the Bible."

—Thomas Jefferson: "The studious perusal of the Sacred Volume will make better citizens, better fathers, and better husbands."

—Andrew Jackson: "The Bible is the rack on which our republic rests."

—Abraham Lincoln: "All the things desirable to men are contained in the Bible."

The Bible and Democracy

The pillars of American democratic law are rooted in the Bible. Before American freedom was won and the Constitution adopted, the principles of democracy were at work in the self-governing churches of the Pilgrims and Puritans. Their church government was modeled upon the New Testament.

Bible quotations are found on America's most revered monuments. The historic Liberty Bell, now in Philadelphia's Independence Hall, bears this inscription from Leviticus 25: 10: "Proclaim liberty throughout all the land unto all the inhabitants thereof."

The United States national motto, "In God We Trust," is inscribed on all coins and the one-dollar bill. Proposed by Reverend Mark R. Watkinson, it is supposed to have been inspired by a line of the National Anthem:

> *"Then conquer we must,*
> *When our cause it is just*
> *And this be our motto:*
> *In God is our trust!"*

And still there is no end to the influence of the Bible.

The Bible and Literature

Consider literature: No self-respecting author in any field of knowledge would be without a copy of the Bible on his desk. The great masters of English and American literature have all dipped into the Bible for inspiration, ideas, and plots. One man made a list of 1,065 titles of English books of fiction, drama, and poetry, not written for religious purposes. He noted that 254 of the titles were quotations or adaptations from the words of Jesus.

Stevenson, Defoe, Dickens, Chaucer, Shakespeare, Milton, Browning, Kipling are only a few of the famous English writers who were influenced by the Bible.

The same is true of Longfellow, Whittier, Bryant, Van Dyke, Lowell, and many other American literary greats.

The most famous travel writer of all time, John Bunyan, based his allegory, *Pilgrim's Progress,* upon the Bible. General Lew Wallace wrote the famous Christian classic, *Ben-Hur,* and in his Biblical research became a Christian himself.

The basic philosophy of Carnegie's book, *How to Win Friends and Influence People* is from Proverbs 18: 24, "A man that hath friends must show himself friendly."

No wonder 50 leading American citizens declared the Bible to be the "Number One piece of literature." A cardinal mark of a great book of literature is the book's influence upon other books.

And still the story is not complete.

The Bible and the Arts

Consider art: The world's greatest masterpieces of painting and sculpture are artists' imaginations of Bible characters.

And music: Bach, Handel, Beethoven, and many other great composers were inspired by the Bible.

And movies: Hollywood has climbed on the Bible band wagon and adapted Bible stories to the screen, although too often the Bible record has been distorted by moviemakers.

And radio and television: Every week hundreds of Biblical sermons and dramas are heard and seen

70

by millions. Billy Graham's "Hour of Decision" is broadcast over about 1,000 stations.

There is simply no end to the influence and impact of the Bible. Through this wonderful Book, God has spoken, and the message has been heard— through preaching, teaching, reading, drama, literature, art, government, crusades for human betterment, and many other ways.

No other book has effected so great an impact upon humanity.

So testify some of the great men of history:

—Herbert Hoover: "We are indebted to the Book of books for our national ideals and institutions. Their preservation rests in adhering to its principles."

—Harry S. Truman: "The Bible is the moral code of civilization."

—Daniel Webster: "The Bible is our only safe guide."

—William James: "The Bible contains more true sublimity, more exquisite beauty, more morality, more important history, and finer strains of poetry and eloquence than can be collected from all other books, in whatever age or language they may have been written."

—Napoleon Bonaparte: "The Bible is no mere book, but a living Power that conquers all that opposes it."

—Sir William E. Gladstone (Prime Minister of

Great Britain): "I have known 95 great men of the world in my time, and of these, 87 were followers of the Bible."

—Sir Isaac Newton (father of modern space travel): "We account the Scriptures of God to be the most sublime philosophy. I find more sure marks of authority in the Bible than in any profane history whatever."

—John Quincy Adams: "The Bible is the Book of all others to read at all ages and in all conditions of human life; not to be read once, or twice, or thrice through, and then laid aside; but to be read in small portions of one or two chapters a day, and never to be omitted by some overwhelming necessity."

—Immanuel Kant: "The existence of the Bible, as a Book for the people, is the greatest benefit which the human race has ever experienced."

—John Ruskin: "All that I have ever taught of art, everything that I have written, whatever greatness there has been in any thought of mine, whatever I have done in my life, has simply been due to the fact that, when I was a child, my mother daily read with me a part of the Bible, and daily made me learn a part of it by heart."

CHAPTER 5

IT CHANGES PEOPLE AND THUS CHANGES THINGS

During World War II a sailor was unloading a crate off a ship. "What is it?" an officer asked.

"Bombs," the sailor replied with a smile.

The officer sprang into action. "Clear the docks!" he shouted. "Get the demolition squad!"

"But, Sir," the sailor stammered. "I was only kidding. This is only a crate of Bibles."

As the officer warily walked toward the crate, the sailor added, lamely, "The Bible IS an explosive force, you know."

The officer didn't appreciate the sailor's joke, but the sailor was right in the sense that the Bible is like a bomb, exploding the inspired message of God into the minds of men, and clearing a path for the entrance of faith. "The Gospel," Paul declares, "is the power of God unto salvation to every one that believeth" (Romans 1: 16). The Greek word translated "power" is *dunamis*, from which came our English word, dynamite. *Dunamis* is, according to *Thayer's Greek-English Lexicon*, "inherent

power residing in a thing by virtue of its nature."
The Bible, in itself, is not a magic or occult book,
but by virtue of divine inspiration, it results in
explosive power when believed and applied.

In every century the Bible has been the target
of attack. A prominent skeptic in 19th century
England challenged a minister to debate the Bible
in a public meeting. The minister agreed upon
one condition: "That you, Sir, will bring two witnesses who have been bettered by believing what
you teach. I will bring 100 witnesses whose lives
have been transformed by believing the message
of the Bible."

The skeptic promptly withdrew, saying, "I cannot meet that condition."

The conclusive evidence of the Bible's superior-
ity over all other books is the transformation of
those who believe and apply its message. What
other book could turn headhunters into missionaries and cause murderous tribes to become peace
loving?

Chief Tariri of Peru

For example, there is the true story of Chief
Tariri, a notorious Peruvian headhunter who had
killed ten chiefs plus an uncounted number of
common jungle Indians. Tariri controlled by terror a large region in the heart of Peru's Amazon
basin. No white man dared enter Tariri's domain.

Even the Peruvian army stayed clear of the murderous chieftain. But two young Wycliffe Bible Translators, Loretta Anderson and Doris Cox, came armed only with Bibles and translator tools. Because they called him "brother," Tariri welcomed them and allowed them to study the language and translate portions of the Bible. Their first convert was Tariri, who not only renounced his murderous ways, but became a missionary to his own tribe.

Tariri came to the New York World's Fair on Peru's Independence Day, July 28, 1966. He declared simply, "I came to tell you about the God I have read about in the Bible." Then he pressed a switch that lighted the Tower of Light, said to be the most powerful artificial light ever constructed, as a symbol of the light that has come to Tariri's tribe through the Bible. About 200 of Tariri's tribesmen have become Christians and for the first time a government school is operating in his village.

Perhaps a more awe-inspiring story than Tariri's comes from the jungles of Ecuador. Ten years ago the world was shocked to hear that five young United States missionaries had been brutally speared to death while trying to make contact with the savage Aucas. The Aucas, like Chief Tariri's Shaphra tribe, had known only war and witchcraft. After the murders, the wife of one of the martyrs and the sister of another were permitted to live with the tribe.

Within a few years all five living killers of the missionaries became Christians. Today the Auca village of Tiwaeno is peaceful and happy. The Auca church ("God's Speaking House") sits in a prominent place. Here about 80 Auca Christians assemble to sing joyful hymns and study the Bible ("God's Carving") in their own language. The leaders of the church are the warriors who killed the five missionaries. Recently one of the killers baptized the teenage son and daughter of the martyred pilot, Nate Saint.

Servicemen and the Bible

Many United States servicemen discovered firsthand evidence of the power of the Bible as they traveled to remote islands in the Pacific. One soldier met a native carrying a Bible who could converse in English. The soldier pointed to the Bible and grinned knowingly. "We educated people don't put much faith in that Book anymore," he said. The islander grinned back. "Well, it's a good thing for you that we do," he said while patting his stomach, "or else, you'd be in here by now."

Hundreds of servicemen became Christians while studying the Bible during World War II and the Korean War. Some returned home to train for the ministry and missionary service. Jacob DeShazer was one.

Sergeant DeShazer was bombardier for one of the planes in General Doolittle's famous squadron. His plane ran out of gas after dumping bombs on Nagoya, Japan, and the crew parachuted into enemy territory.

DeShazer and the other crewmen were put into a prison camp. He passed the time in a five-foot-wide cell and was allowed out for exercise only a few moments each morning. Then a Bible was given to the captured fliers. They took turns reading. DeShazer's turn came last because he ranked lowest.

Although he had the Bible for only three weeks, he read it through and memorized dozens of key verses. After reading Romans 10: 9, he trusted in Christ. Later he said, "My heart was full of joy. I wouldn't have traded places with anyone."

Now he felt only love for his cruel guards. When a guard slapped him, slammed the cell door on his bare foot, and began kicking at the foot with hobnailed boots, DeShazer said nothing, but thought of Jesus' words, "Love your enemies" (Matthew 5:44). After this the guard became friendly.

When the war was over, Jacob DeShazer prepared for missionary service. He went back to Japan and met some of his old prison guards. Two told him, "We want to become Christians." De-Shazer smiled in reply. "Now we can love one another."

The story of Jacob DeShazer's conversion and return to Japan was printed in a tract. Mitsuo Fuchida, the Japanese officer who had led the attack on Pearl Harbor, read the story and sought out Christian missionaries. Today both Fuchida and DeShazer are teaching the Bible to the Japanese people.

The United States servicemen who were imprisoned on Corregidor will never forget the horrors of that camp, but even there the Bible proved to be powerful.

The Japanese permitted each American prisoner to carry only one blanket into the prison camp. Instead of a blanket one soldier carried a Bible wrapped in canvas. He had found the Bible in a bombed-out Philippine chapel.

The soldier carried the Bible on the terrifying death marches which took the lives of many prisoners. He took it on the prison ships and finally into the terrible camp at Cabanatuan. There he gave the Bible to the prisoners' church.

What was the result?

The American Bible Society reports that the Book was read Sunday after Sunday to sick and half-starved men by the chaplains. Many received hope in Christ before succumbing to diseases and starvation. By the end of the war, 1,500 prisoners had declared their faith in Christ and received Christian baptism.

The Hope of Suffering Mankind

No other book offers so much hope to suffering mankind as the Bible. The only hospital in the continental United States for sufferers of Hansen's disease (called leprosy by some) is in Carville, Louisiana. Here, the Protestant chaplain introduced me to the members of his flock. I met sightless "Brother Brady" who has been a patient since 1925. "Brother Brady," an avid student of the Bible, summed up his life in two terse sentences: "Once I could see but I was blind to spiritual things. Now I am blind but I can see."

In the occupational ward I met Anna, an aged Negro woman with shining silver hair. Her face was deformed and the disease had taken one leg. She was weaving a colorful pattern of cloth. When the chaplain mentioned that she sung in the choir, I asked if she would sing a verse of her favorite hymn. Her lips moved and a deep-throated burst of song rushed out: *"I sing because I'm happy; I sing because I'm free!"* Then she began a second hymn and our eyes brimmed with tears as she sang, "Never Give Up."

One evening I sat in the services of Chicago's Pacific Garden Mission located amidst the squalor of seedy flophouses, cheap saloons, and lusty burlesque houses. The old "Lighthouse" rang with hallelujahs as men quoted Scripture and told how they had been transformed. Bible verses in large letters on the walls declared the message of hope for hopeless men. Here, I knew, thousands of men had found new life from believing the message of the old Book. Many of the stories have been dramatically told on the radio program "Unshackled."

Mel Trotter had been on his way to jump in the icy waters of Lake Michigan when he wandered into the mission. An impossible drunkard, he had come home from a ten-day spree to find his baby son dead in his wife's arms. Then he had cried out, "I'm a murderer. I'll end my life." And he had set out to do it.

At the mission on State Street he heard Harry Monroe, the superintendent, tell how the God of the Bible had given him forgiveness and new hope in life. The despondent husband hung grimly onto every promise of the Bible that was quoted. When Monroe said, "Jesus loves you. Make room in your heart for Him tonight," Mel Trotter stumbled forward. Three years later, Trotter was appointed superintendent of a rescue mission in Grand Rapids, Michigan. This became a base for him to start 55 other lighthouses in the United States—all to present the Bible message of hope to the down-and-outer.

"Dad" Brinkley greeted me from his prison cell on death row in Houston, Texas. He had been sentenced to the electric chair for killing his wife, a crime he had committed while drunk. To the prison came Reverend E. A. Munroe. He sat with the convicted killer and read, "Though your sins be as scarlet, they shall be as white as snow" (Isaiah 1: 18). After more Bible verses were read, "Dad" Brinkley knelt and cried for forgiveness and mercy.

As I spoke with him and asked, "How are you?" he smiled and said, "For the first time in my life, I have peace in my soul. If it's God's will for me to die, then I'm ready. I'm looking forward to meeting my loved ones in Heaven." We prayed together, then the guard led Lonnie Brinkley back to his cell. He walked tall and erect with the dignity of a man set free.

The Bible Changes Lives

The Bible—when read and taught—has always left in its trail monuments of divine grace. Murderers, drunkards, thieves, immoral men, and other sinners have found forgiveness, release from guilt, and a purpose in living from responding to the message of God's Book. Indeed, some who have been pulled from the depths of degradation are now ranked among the greatest leaders of the Church.

Aurelius Augustine, fourth-century Latin scholar and pagan, is one example. Though convinced that the Bible was an inspired Book, he felt unable to overcome his sinful passions. He wrestled with his fears until one day in a garden he flung himself down under a fig tree, and cried, "O Lord, make an end of my vileness!"

That moment he heard a child's voice crying *"Tolle lege! Tolle lege!* Take and read! Take and read!" He took the voice to be a command to open the Bible and read. He grasped a copy of Romans lying nearby and read the first passage. His eyes fell upon: "Let us walk honestly, as in the day; not in rioting and drunkenness, not in chambering and wantonness, not in strife and envying. But put ye on the Lord Jesus Christ, and make not provision for the flesh, to fulfill the lusts thereof" (Romans 13: 13, 14). Suddenly he cried to a friend, "I have put on Christ! My heart glows with the light of peace!" This was the man who became the Bible's most influential interpreter in the Roman Empire. His *Confessions*, which are filled with Bible quotations, ranks today as one of the 100 greatest books of all time.

Conversely, enemies of the Bible have been stricken down by its message then raised by God's power to proclaim as truth the very Book they once opposed. During the Civil War Captain Russell Conwell saw his personal aide reading the

Bible and screamed, "Put that away. I gave up such foolishness long ago. As your superior officer, I command you to stop."

The aide, Johnny Ring, never obeyed that command although he later gave his life while trying to rescue Captain Conwell's sword during a battle. The memory of Johnny Ring reading the Bible haunted Conwell until in a hospital he surrendered his life to Christ. After the war he founded the *Minneapolis Chronicle* (now the *Tribune*), then became a minister and built the huge Temple Baptist Church, seating 4,000, in Philadelphia. He founded the great Temple University, a hospital, wrote dozens of books, and received over 6,000 previously non-Christians into his church.

Great Men and the Bible

Millions of lives have been transformed by believing and heeding the message of the Bible. Most do not lend themselves to dramatic telling. But their daily living bears a telling testimony that the Bible is true.

Some of these "quiet people" are leaders in national life. Some are scientists, doctors, university professors, and professional athletes.

To mention a few of the better known people who have experienced the power of the Bible in their lives:

—Honorable Mark O. Hatfield, Governor of Oregon, a Baptist Sunday school teacher and crusading layman: "I believe II Corinthians 5: 15: 'And that he (Christ) died for all, that they which live should not henceforth live unto themselves, but unto him which died for them, and rose again,' and Hebrews 13: 6: 'The Lord is my helper, and I will not fear what man shall do unto me.' "

—James F. Oates, Jr., Chairman of the Board, the Equitable Life Assurance Society: "It is the extraordinary and commanding quality in so many instances of a verse to reflect with exact accuracy our own inner innate beliefs and aspirations. It is this inspiration stimulated within which irrevocably establishes—at least to my satisfaction—the true believability of the Scriptures."

—G. Tom Willey, missile expert and vice-president of the Martin Company: "As a boy of 16 I listened to a sermon on that wonderful verse, 'For God so loved the world, that he gave his only begotten Son, that whosoever believeth in him should not perish, but have everlasting life' (John 3: 16). The best I knew how I put my hand in the nail-pierced hand of the Savior, and God took up the count for me."

—Lt. General William K. Harrison, former Senior Delegate to the United Nations Command Truce Team in Korea: "In the Bible, the Word of God, the Lord has promised that anyone who believes in His only begotten Son, the Lord Jesus Christ,

84

has been forgiven his sin and its consequences, has been given eternal life and has entered forever into the Kingdom of God. God has done this for me."

—Ulric Jelinek, inventor and president of the Severna Manufacturing Corporation: "Since I became a Christian at 15, I've had an unusual hunger for God's Word. My habit is to read the Bible through once each year. I always find something startlingly new. I'm interested in new knowledge. What scientist isn't?"

Miss America Carried a Bible

—Vonda Kay Van Dyke, Miss America of 1965: When being interviewed during the Miss America pageant finals, she was asked "Do you carry a Bible as a good luck charm?" The 21-year-old Sunday school teacher replied, "It's not a charm, but the most important Book I own." Later at a Billy Graham Crusade, she added, "I found out (from the Bible) that it wasn't enough to give God your talents, or to attend church and Sunday school. You need to give Him your whole life."

—John E. Mitchell, Jr., President of John E. Mitchell Company, Machinery Manufacturers: "There are not many things in life that I can be sure about. But, thank God, I can be, and am sure about the things that count. I am sure that

Almighty God has spoken to man through His Word, the Bible."

—Bill Wade, quarterback, Chicago Bears Football Club: "When I accepted Christ, there came an inward peace and thirst for spiritual things. I began to pray and study the Bible more than I ever had."

—Raymond Berry, pass receiver, Baltimore Colts Football Club: "After I accepted Christ, studying the Word of God became a real joy, and verses that before had no meaning suddenly did have meaning."

—Felipe Alou, outfielder, Atlanta Braves Baseball Club: "For a long time in my hotel room I meditated upon Romans 10:13—'For whosoever shall call upon the name of the Lord shall be saved.' 'I have called upon Christ,' I told myself. 'He has promised to accept me.' Suddenly the light dawned and I said, 'I am a Christian! I belong to Christ!' "

—Allen Worthington, pitcher, Minnesota Twins Baseball Club: "I was on the plane and reading my Bible when I came to John 9:39 where Jesus said, 'I am come into this world, that they which see not might see; and that they which see might be made blind.' Suddenly my eyes were opened. I saw that Christ was my Savior, that He had forgiven all my sins, that in Him I possessed a brand new life. From that moment the Bible became a beautiful Book to me."

"The Bible Is My Rule Book"

—Clendon Thomas, football All-American, defensive back, Pittsburgh Steelers Football Club: "The Bible is my rule book. From it I learn that I am a sinner and that Christ died for my sins. I learn how to live in daily fellowship with God and how to be victorious over the temptations of Satan."

—Honorable Eugene Siler, Representative of the Eighth Congressional District of Kentucky: "One of my favorite Bible texts is the story of the conversion of Zacchaeus—Luke 19: 1-10. Here is a man who ran, repented, and received salvation. His story is proof that God is even interested in saving politicians."

—Dr. Edson Peck, Associate Professor of Physics, Northwestern University: "My church once invited me to conduct a three-month study on science and the Bible. I was happy to do it. Many Christians have a vague feeling that science and the Bible conflict. I was glad to assure my fellow church members that that is not true."

—Walter F. Burke, general manager of Project Mercury and Gemini, and vice-president of the McDonnell Aircraft Corporation: "I have found nothing in science or space exploration to compel me to throw away my Bible or to reject my Savior, Jesus Christ, in whom I trust. The space age has been a factor in the deepening of my own spiritual life. I read the Bible more now. I get from the

Bible what I cannot get from science—the really important things of life."

—John Hedges, automobile dealer, who puts a New Testament with this letter in the glove compartment of every automobile he sells: "Please accept our gift of this small New Testament. It is given to you because it has been a help to so many millions . . . What you do with this Book is your choice, but its direction for living can be as important as the road map you may also carry in your glove compartment."

—Dr. Elmer W. Engstrom, chief executive officer and chairman of the Executive Committee, Radio Corporation of America: "From my business experience I have clearly learned the necessity of having a charter of one's operations and following that charter in total belief and commitment. In the Christian life and in the church, the Bible is our charter—the supreme authority for life. We need to accept it by faith and ask for understanding. Then we need to make Christ the Lord of our whole lives."

—Marion E. Wade, founder and chairman of the board of directors, Wade-Wenger ServiceMaster* Co.: "I was especially drawn to Joshua 1: 8, which says, 'This book of the law shall not depart out of thy mouth; but thou shalt meditate therein day and night, that thou mayest observe to do accord-

* Registered trademark.

ing to all that is written therein: for then thou shalt make thy way prosperous, and then thou shalt have good *success*.' Later I found that this is the only place in the Bible where the word success appears. The truth hit me that I could only succeed with God, my fellow man, and myself by living according to the Bible."

These testimonies and others reveal that through the pages of the world's best seller God Himself speaks to anyone who is willing to listen.

The greatest "wonder" of the Bible is the wonder of what God can do to those who will believe and apply the life-changing Message of the Word.

BIBLIOGRAPHY

The Bible: Its Significance and Authority

Brunner, E., *Revelation and Reason,* tr. Olive Wyon, Philadelphia: Westminster Press, 1946.

Colwell, E. C., *The Study of the Bible,* Chicago: University of Chicago Press, 1937.

Dodd, C. H., *The Authority of the Bible,* New York: Harper & Row, 1929.

Goodspeed, E. J., *The Story of the Bible,* Chicago: University of Chicago Press, 1936.

Kenyon, F. G., *Our Bible and the Ancient Manuscripts,* New York: Harper & Row, 1940.

Kenyon, F. G., *The Text of the Greek Bible,* London: Duckworth, 1947.

Pfeiffer, R. H., *Introduction to the Old Testament,* New York: Harper & Row, 1941.

Price, I. M., *The Ancestry of Our English Bible: An Account of Manuscripts, Texts, and Versions of the Bible,* ed. W. A. Irwin and Allen Wikgren, New York: Harper & Row, 1949.

Richardson, A., *Preface to Bible Study,* Philadelphia: Westminster Press, 1944.

Rowley, H. H., ed., *The Old Testament and Modern Study,* Oxford: Clarendon Press, 1951.

Schweitzer, A., *The Quest of the Historical Jesus,* tr. W. Montgomery, New York: Macmillan, 1950.

Souter, A., *The Text and Canon of the New Testament,* New York: Charles Scribner's Sons, 1913.

Tesh, S. E., *How We Got Our Bible,* Cincinnati: Standard, 1951.

91

The Bible: Selected Books for Personal Bible Study

Cruden, A., *Cruden's Unabridged Concordance*, Grand Rapids: Baker Book House, rev. ed. 1954.

Davis, S. D., *The Westminster Dictionary of the Bible*, Philadelphia: Westminster Press, 1944.

Halley, H. H., *Halley's Bible Handbook*, Grand Rapids: Zondervan, rev. ed. 1962.

Henry, M., and Scott, T., *Concise Commentary on the Whole Bible*, Chicago: Moody Press, rev. ed. 1966.

Joy, C. R., *Harper's Topical Concordance*, New York: Harper and Row, rev. ed. 1962.

Nave, O. J., *Nave's Topical Bible*, Chicago: Moody Press.

Pfeiffer, C. F., *Baker's Bible Atlas*, Grand Rapids: Baker Book House, 1961.

Pfeiffer, C. F., and Harrison, E. F., *Wycliffe Bible Commentary*, Chicago: Moody Press, 1962.

Smith, W., *New Smith's Bible Dictionary*, Grand Rapids: Zondervan, rev. ed. 1966.

Tenney, M. C., *Zondervan Pictorial Bible Dictionary*, Grand Rapids: Zondervan, 1963.

Terrien, S., *Golden Bible Atlas*, New York: Golden Press, 1957.

Wright, G. E., and Filson, F. V., *Westminster Historical Atlas to the Bible*, Philadelphia: Westminster Press, rev. ed. 1956.

How About You?
Have You Read These Yet?

THE VIEW FROM A HEARSE, by Joseph Bayly

Death is never popular; it's the last thing most people want to talk about. But it's there, always there, waiting. Waiting to claim parent, child, husband, wife, lover, friend — and me. Accident or cancer or bullet or bomb: death has many doors.

The View from a Hearse answers questions about death. It does not seek to comfort, but to present facts . . . some of them chilling. The author does not stop with cold information about death, however. He also answers the centuries-old question, "If a man dies, shall he live again?" The fabric of hope is skillfully woven throughout.

YOU KNOW I CAN'T HEAR YOU WHEN YOU ACT THAT WAY, by Bill Eakin and Jack Hamilton

For these days when young people are plagued with serious questions about church, morals, government, religion, and life in general, this book addresses itself to questions teens are asking.

Using questions actually asked by today's young people as the basis for their comments, authors Bill Eakin and Jack Hamilton have expressed themselves in readable and friendly style to the serious questions of today's world.